modern readers — stage 4

Seeds of Love

Eduardo Amos
Elisabeth Prescher
Ernesto Pasqualin

2nd edition

Richmond

© EDUARDO AMOS, ELISABETH PRESCHER, ERNESTO PASQUALIN, 2005

Richmond

Diretoria: *Paul Berry*
Gerência editorial: *Sandra Possas*
Coordenação de *bureau*: *Américo Jesus*
Coordenação de pesquisa iconográfica: *Ana Lucia Soares*
Coordenação de revisão: *Estevam Vieira Lédo Jr.*
Coordenação de produção gráfica: *André Monteiro, Maria de Lourdes Rodrigues*
Coordenação de produção industrial: *Wilson Troque*

Projeto editorial: *Sandra Possas, Kylie Mackin*

Assistência editorial: *Gabriela Peixoto Vilanova*
Revisão: *Maria Cecília Kinker Caliendo*
Projeto gráfico de miolo e capa: *Ricardo Van Steen Comunicações e
  Propaganda Ltda./Oliver Fuchs*
Edição de arte: *Christiane Borin*
Ilustrações de miolo e capa: *Rogério Borges*
Diagramação: *Formato Comunicação*
Pré-impressão: *Helio P. de Souza Filho, Marcio H. Kamoto*
Impressão e acabamento: Bercrom Gráfica e Editora
Lote: 283297

Dados Internacionais de Catalogação na Publicação (CIP)
(Câmara Brasileira do Livro, SP, Brasil)

Amos, Eduardo
  Seeds of love / Eduardo Amos, Elisabeth Prescher,
Ernesto Pasqualin. — 2. ed. — São Paulo : Moderna, 2004. —
[Modern readers ; stage 4]

  1. Inglês (Ensino fundamental) I. Prescher, Elisabeth.
II. Pasqualin, Ernesto. III. Título. IV. Série.

04-0907   CDD-372.652

Índices para catálogo sistemático:
1. Inglês : Ensino fundamental   372.652

ISBN 85-16-04092-5

Reprodução proibida. Art. 184 do Código Penal e Lei 9.610 de 19 de fevereiro de 1998.

Todos os direitos reservados.

RICHMOND
EDITORA MODERNA LTDA.
Rua Padre Adelino, 758 — Belenzinho
São Paulo — SP — Brasil — CEP 03303-904
www.richmond.com.br
2019

Impresso no Brasil

Chapter 1

Planet Earth. Year 3052.

The supercivilized people of the planet live in Tower-Cities built 2,220 meters above the ground.

Below the Tower-Cities is the Underworld – the ruins of civilizations that lived on earth before the Big Change, many centuries ago.

There is only one country now – UNICOM (Universal Community). The Council of Elders, called the Guardians of the Peace, governs UNICOM.

One morning, some students were learning about the beginning of Unicom at their computer terminals in the Education Center.

One of the boys, Akron Matenko, asked many questions.

GIVE ME SOME INFORMATION ABOUT THE GUARDIANS OF THE PEACE.
Guardians of the Peace: The most important people in our civilization.
Number of Guardians of the Peace on the Council: 150
Duties: To establish UNICOM rules and regulations.

Akron asked if he could become a Guardian of Peace one day. Then, the screen displayed a list of requirements.

REQUIREMENTS
Age: At least 120 years old.
Personal qualities: Must be mature and wise.
Educational background: 55 years (including meditation, non-verbal communication, extrasensory perception).

WHO WERE THE GUARDIANS OF PEACE BEFORE THE BIG CHANGE?

INFORMATION NOT AVAILABLE!!!

BUT I WANT TO KNOW!!!

INFORMATION NOT AVAILABLE. CLASS OVER.
GOOD-BYE, AKRON MATENKO.

"It isn't fair! This computer never tells me what I want to know."

"You can't argue with computers," said a girl.

"Be careful, Akron. The Central System knows everything," remarked a boy.

"But I want to know. I have the right to know," replied Akron angrily.

They looked at Akron and left the room.

Gea, a girl who was at the back of the room, came up to him and said, "Don't be sad, Akron. The same thing happened to me last year. Maybe you want to know something that it is better not to know."

The screen started to flash.

MESSAGE FOR AKRON MATENKO

GO TO SECTOR BC-03 IMMEDIATELY.
TALK TO ELDER AVROHOM.

Chapter 2

There was no one in the reception area when Akron got to the Reeducation Center. But, after a while, a green sign lit up at the top of a door: ADMISSION ALLOWED!

"Did you call for me, Elder Avrohom?" Akron asked when he entered.

"Yes, I did," said the old man. "I want to talk to you, Akron. This isn't the first time you've asked about the time before the Big Change."

Akron blushed.

"The information you want is confidential." The old man looked at the boy kindly and added, "But I will tell you something about it."

Avrohom explained that before the Big Change, the planet was divided into countries. Each country had its own guardian.

"What's the mystery, then?" asked Akron.

"The guardians had different interests and fought. They didn't care about peace or the people's welfare. They were guided by greed and envy. The world was filled with hunger and poverty."

"I have another question, Elder Avrohom," said the boy.

"That's enough. Forget about those days. All you need to know is that we created a new civilization. In this civilization, there's no war. We live in peace and harmony. That's what matters."

"But..."

"Your time is over. Go now, my boy," said Avrohom.

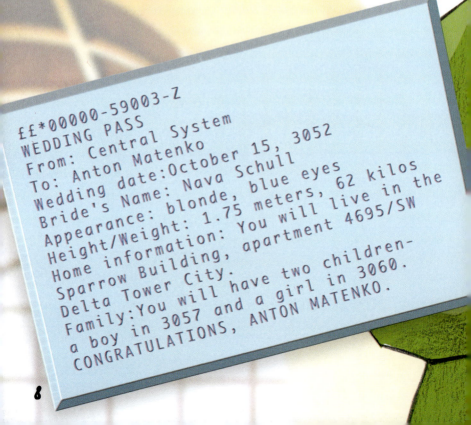

££*00000-59003-Z
WEDDING PASS
From: Central System
To: Anton Matenko
Wedding date: October 15, 3052
Bride's Name: Nava Schull
Appearance: blonde, blue eyes
Height/Weight: 1.75 meters, 62 kilos
Home information: You will live in the Sparrow Building, apartment 4695/SW Delta Tower City.
Family: You will have two children- a boy in 3057 and a girl in 3060.
CONGRATULATIONS, ANTON MATENKO.

When Akron got home, his brother was very excited.
"What's up, Anton?" Akron asked.
"I'm very happy. I'm going to get married. I received my wedding pass today. Look!"

"That's nice, Anton!" said Akron.

"Nice? You said nice? It's wonderful!" replied Anton. "What about you? Any news?"

"Yes, I'm going to the Underworld. My class is going on a field trip the day after tomorrow."

"Great! I remember when I went there with my class."

"Did you like it?" asked Akron.

"Sure. It's interesting, but a little dangerous," said Anton. "Stay close to your group and never enter a Red Zone."

Akron listened to his brother attentively.

"I still have my laser flashlight. I can lend it to you. It's very useful in the Underworld."

"Thanks, Anton. I'm sure I'll need it."

 Chapter 3

The trip down to the Underworld was long and slow.

"Turn on your flashlights and stay close together," said the guide.

Soon, they were walking around the dark ruins. The guide stopped in front of a three-story building with large windows.

"This used to be a school," he said. "We are going inside now. You can walk around freely, but don't enter the Red Zone."

The students visited the science laboratory and the art room. Then, they entered a regular classroom with desks and a blackboard.

"Where are the computers? Who taught the students?" asked a boy.

"The teachers did," answered the guide. "They talked to the students; they asked and answered questions."

"The students were lucky," said Akron. "I have a computer, but it doesn't tell me what I want to know."

Everybody laughed. They left the classroom and walked along a hallway. A sign above a door attracted their attention.

"This is a Red Zone – a forbidden area," said the guide. Ancient humans used to write their history in books. As you know, books contain useless and dangerous information and are forbidden in UNICOM."

Akron didn't hear a word of what the guide was saying. When he saw the door, he started to feel strange – his hands sweated and his body trembled.

"I know the answers to my questions are right here," he thought. "I have to see what is inside."

At the end of the day, the group camped outside a big warehouse. Everybody was tired and fell asleep quickly. Everyone, except Akron. He was too excited to sleep.

Akron took his laser flashlight and silently left his tent. He ran to the school building and went to the door with the "RED ZONE" sign.

The door wasn't locked. He pushed it open and entered the room very carefully.

Akron walked along the shelves covered by thousands of books.

He was so fascinated that he lost track of time. When he looked out of the window, the sun was rising.

"Daylight already!" he said aloud. "I'd better go back."

He grabbed a book from a shelf and ran back to the camp.

Chapter 4

After the trip to the Underworld, Akron read the book over and over.

"...You can only see clearly with your heart."

Akron had already read this line from the book ten times. "What does it mean?" he asked himself.

He decided to ask his computer.

DEFINITION OF HEART

Heart: A hollow muscular organ in vertebrate animals.
YOU CAN ONLY SEE CLEARLY WITH YOUR HEART.
ERROR. YOU CAN ONLY SEE CLEARLY WITH YOUR EYES.
NO. MY SENTENCE IS NOT WRONG! TELL ME WHAT IT MEANS!
YOUR SENTENCE IS WRONG. DO NOT INSIST. FROM NOW ON, THIS TERMINAL IS UNDER SURVEILLANCE.

The computer shut itself off.

Akron's friends began to notice that there was something wrong with him. He was always quiet. Gea was the only person he talked to. Everybody thought that he was sick.

He himself noticed that something unusual was happening to him. Sometimes his heart beat quickly and his hands trembled. At other times, he felt his throat go dry.

"What is happening to me?" he thought. "Why do I sometimes feel so sad and insecure? And why do I feel so happy at times? Maybe it is the book... maybe it is Gea. The symptoms come back every time she is around."

One day, after class, Akron and Gea were the only students left in the classroom.

"Gea, I have to talk to you," said Akron.

He told her about the Underworld and his symptoms.

"You're crazy!" she said. "You know Red Zones are forbidden areas. And your symptoms, when did they start?"

"They started after I read the book," he said. "But I have the symptoms when you are around, too. Here's the book, Gea! Read it and tell me what you think."

"You are really crazy, Akron," Gea said, "but I'll read it."

That afternoon, Gea was in her bedroom. She was holding the book, but she was not reading it. She was thinking about Akron.

"Akron is wrong," she thought. "It is not the book. I haven't read it yet, but I have the same symptoms. I tremble when he is around, and I blush when he looks at me. Something is happening to us and we have to find out what it is."

She looked at the book and started to read.

"Akron, I have to talk to you," said Gea when she saw him at the Education Center the next morning.

"Is it about the book?" he asked.

"Yes, well... Remember what you told me about your symptoms? Well, I feel the same thing. But it's not because of the book. It's because of you. You make me feel like this."

"Really?" he asked.

"Yes. I read the book and I'm confused now. I'm afraid, Akron."

"We have to go to the Underworld," Akron whispered. "I'm sure the answer is there."

"I agree, but how can we go there?" asked Gea. "The Central System controls all visits to the Underworld."

"I know, but I'll find a way to go back there," he said.

Chapter 5

GUIDES NEEDED
FIELD TRIP TO THE UNDERWORLD
DEPARTURE: THURSDAY AT 3:00 P.M.
DURATION: 2 DAYS
INFORMATION AT THE EDUCATION CENTER

When the 3-D screen showed the advertisement asking for guides, Akron rushed to the phone and called Gea.

"This is our chance," he said. "Meet me at the Education Center."

On Thursday afternoon, several groups of students went down to the Underworld. Akron and Gea were among them.

It was very dark and silent in the camp area when Akron left his tent to meet Gea.

"Let's go! Quick!" said Akron.

Akron ran through the dusty streets to the school building. Gea followed him very closely.

"I'm scared," she said when they arrived at the RED ZONE. "If they find us here..."

"They won't wake up until 7:00 in the morning. We have about eight hours," Akron said. Then, he opened the door and they stepped in.

They spent the first hour wandering around.

Dusty shelves crowded with books filled the large room.

"Wow! There are thousands of books here," said Gea. "How are we going to find what we are looking for?"

"Remember our extrasensory perception classes?" said Akron. "Close your eyes and let your hands guide you."

The minutes which followed were magical and mysterious. Their hands touched centuries of stories and emotions. They could feel the essence of each book, the emotions of each writer.

All of a sudden, Gea's hands stopped at an ancient leather-bound volume.

"Here it is!" she whispered.

They sat in a large armchair and read the book together. They discovered that in the old days people felt hatred, jealousy, and envy, but also love.

When they finished the book, they were both moved. They finally understood what was happening to them.

They looked at each other but they didn't say anything. Then, they slowly moved closer and closer together. Their lips touched in a soft kiss. They were in love.

Chapter 6

Back at UNICOM, Akron and Gea could hardly hide their feelings. Their friends thought that they were different and asked if something was wrong with them. Akron and Gea, however, did not say a word.

Their feelings were making them enjoy things in a new way. Their parents soon noticed the difference.

SPECIAL MESSAGE FROM THE COUNCIL OF ELDERS

189211

14805

Gea Braasch

Akron Matenko

REPORT TO THE COUNCIL OF ELDERS.
PUBLIC HEARING TOMORROW AT 7:00 P.M.

One morning, Gea gave her father a big hug as she was leaving for the Education Center. He was surprised.

"Strange things are happening to our daughter," he told his wife.

"Yes, I noticed that too. Maybe she's sick. Hey, what's that on the 3-D?"

They went to the window and looked at the three-dimensional message in the sky.

The next afternoon, Elder Orr, chairman of the Council of Elders, opened the public hearing with the Fact File for the case.

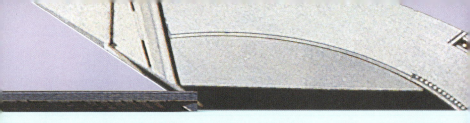

FACT FILE
ACCUSED: AKRON MATENKO   GEA BRAASH

DATE: SEPTEMBER 15   **PLACE:** EDUCATION CENTER
FACT: AKRON TRIED TO OBTAIN CONFIDENTIAL INFORMATION FROM A COMPUTER TERMINAL.

DATE: SEPTEMBER 16   **PLACE:** REEDUCATION CENTER
FACT: AKRON WAS ADVISED BY ELDER AVROHOM.

DATE: SEPTEMBER 28   **PLACE:** UNDERWORLD
FACT: AKRON ENTERED A RED ZONE AND STOLE A DANGEROUS ITEM.

DATE: OCTOBER 2   **PLACE:** HOME
FACT: AKRON ASKED FOR ILLOGICAL INFORMATION FROM HIS HOME COMPUTER.

DATE: OCTOBER 19   **PLACE:** EDUCATION CENTER
FACT: AKRON PASSED THE DANGEROUS ITEM TO SCHOOLMATE GEA BRAASH. GEA TOOK THE DANGEROUS ITEM HOME.

DATE: OCTOBER 21   **PLACE:** UNDERWORLD
FACT: AKRON AND GEA ENTERED A RED ZONE. HAD ANOTHER CONTACT WITH DANGEROUS ITEMS.

CLASSIFICATION: SEVERE OFFENSE

"This is a very serious case," said Elder Gowa, the prosecutor.

"These two youngsters have threatened our civilization. We should sentence them to life imprisonment. They should go to a space jail on a distant satellite."

"I am very sorry to interrupt you, Elder Gowa," said Elder Avrohom. "Please present a more detailed explanation. Please tell these youngsters why they have threatened our civilization."

"They don't deserve an explanation."

"I do insist," said Elder Avrohom. "Your explanation will teach not only these two young people, but also all the people of UNICOM."

"Well, then. Before the Big Change, humans lived at war. There was a lot of hatred and other negative feelings. Our planet was almost destroyed."

He looked at the audience and continued,

"Then, a few brave men created UNICOM, a world of peace and harmony; a world with no countries, no money and no feelings. Now, we have everything we need: food, housing, work, and health care. This is the best period in the history of mankind."

"The Red Zone contains dangerous items. They can bring back ancient feelings and knowledge. We don't need them."

Elder Avrohom turned to Akron and Gea and asked, "Do you understand what you have done? Do you have anything to say?"

Gea stood up very slowly. The large room was in silence.

"The facts are correct, members of the Council," said Gea. "But they don't tell the whole story. I need to tell you about feelings."

"Feelings? Feelings?" Elder Gowa interrupted her. "Don't say such a word! The ancient civilization was destroyed by envy, greed, and hatred. Only reason can guide us!"

Akron stood up and spoke.

"Excuse me, Elder Gowa, but I can't agree with you. Reason and feelings are equally important."

"There are positive feelings like love, for example," Akron said.

"Love can't destroy anything," added Gea. "When you love someone, you feel happy, and you want everybody else to be happy, too."

"Why do you two talk so much about love?" asked Elder Gowa.

Gea stared at the Council members and said in a loud, clear voice, "Because Akron and I are in love."

"OOOOH!!!" gasped the Elders and the audience.

"These youngsters can corrupt our society!" shouted one of the elders.

Akron said, "I don't really care if you send us to jail. Just send us there together and we'll be happy!"

Then, all the Elders started shouting angrily.

Chapter 7

When the room was silent again, Elder Gowa said, "Even love can be dangerous. It can turn into jealousy and hatred. We can't allow that!"

"But," Gea said, "today, at this hearing, you showed some kind of love, your love for Unicom."

"Yes," Akron added." "And Elder Avrohom showed his love for justice."

Akron continued,

"You created the "perfect" civilization. But, without feelings, we can't enjoy it. Your wisdom and experience can help us bring back good feelings."

The members of the Council were touched by the boy's words.

Elder Orr stood up slowly and said, "Members of the Council. I think we are not ready to make a decision now. Let's continue tomorrow at the same time."

35

The public hearing was suspended. Akron and Gea were taken to a Security Building. They would wait there for the next session.

It was going to be a long night for Akron and Gea. But they knew that they had planted seeds of love in the hearts of many people.

Late that night, thousands of people crowded into the elevators that went to the Underworld. It was certainly going to be a long night down there, too. Perhaps the beginning of a new era.

The meaning of each word corresponds to its use in the context of the story (see page number 00)

above (3) acima
advertisement (20) propaganda, anúncio
allowed (7) permitido
angrily (34) com raiva, raivosamente
argue (6) discutir
attentively (10) atentamente
available (5) disponível
background (5) experiência, conhecimento
below (3) abaixo
blush, blushed (7) corar, ficar vermelho
carefully (14) cuidadosamente
century, centuries (3) século
chairman (28) presidente
council (3) conselho
dangerous (10) perigoso
dusty (21) empoeirado
duty, duties (4) dever, obrigação
elder (3) mais velho
envy (8) inveja
extrasensory perception (5) percepção extra-sensorial
field trip (10) excursão
flashlight (10) lanterna
freely (11) livremente

forbidden (13) proibido
gasp, gasped (34) sobressaltar-se
greed (8) ganância
ground (3) solo
guardian (3) guardião
hatred (24) ódio
hide (25) esconder
hollow (15) oco
hunger (8) fome
inside (11) dentro
jail (30) cadeia
jealousy (24) ciúme
kindly (7) gentilmente
laugh, laughed (12) dar risada
mankind (31) humanidade
mature (5) maduro
non-verbal (5) não-verbal
perhaps (36) talvez
poverty (8) pobreza
prosecutor (30) advogado de acusação
reply, replied (6) responder, respondeu
requirement (5) requerimento
ruin (3) ruína
rush, rushed (20) correr
scared (21) com medo
screen (5) tela
seed (36) semente

shelf, shelves (14) prateleira, prateleiras
sign (7) aviso, cartaz
slow (11) devagar
soft (24) macio
step in, stepped in (21) entrar
supercivilized (3) supercivilizado
surveillance (15) vigilância
sweat, sweated (13) suar
threaten, threatened (30) ameaçar
three-story (11) de três andares
throat (16) garganta
tremble, trembled (13) tremer
unusual (16) incomum
useless (13) inútil
wander, wandering (22) vagar
warehouse (14) armazém
wedding (9) casamento
welfare (8) bem-estar
whisper, whispered (19) cochichar

wisdom (35) sabedoria
wise (5) sábio

Expressions

after a while (7) depois de um tempo
All of a sudden (23) De repente
at least (5) pelo menos
Be careful! (6) Tenha cuidado!
came up (6) veio
fell asleep (14) adormeceu
go dry (16) secar
It isn't fair! (6) Não é justo!
leather-bound (23) capa de couro, encapada de couro
life imprisonment (30) prisão perpétua
lit up (7) acendeu
lost track of time (14) perdeu a noção de tempo
That's what matters. (8) É o que importa.

ACTIVITIES

Before Reading

1. Can you imagine life one thousand years from now? What will be different about:

   (the food) (transportation) (human relationships) (housing) (education)

While Reading

Chapter 1

2. Answer the questions below about the Guardians of the Peace.
   a) Who are they?
   b) What are their duties?
   c) What are the requirements to become one?

3. Why didn't the computer answer Akron's questions?

Chapter 2

4. The statements that follow are all wrong. Correct them according to the story.
   a) This is the first time Akron has asked about the Big Change.
   b) People from UNICOM know everything about love.
   c) The guardians were guided by peace and people's welfare.

5. Why was Akron's brother so happy? What is the wedding pass?

Chapter 3

6. Put the sentences in the correct order.
   a) (   ) The students visited the science laboratory.
   b) (   ) They were walking around the dark ruins.
   c) (   ) A sign above a door attracted their attention.
   d) (   ) They entered a regular classroom with desks.
   e) (1) The trip was long and slow.
   f) (   ) They left the classroom and walked along a hallway.

39

7. What is the "Red Zone"?
8. According to the guide, why are books forbidden?

Chapter 4

9. Tick the correct answer.
   a) Akron's symptoms came back when:
      (   ) he was with the book
      (   ) he was near Gea

   b) When Akron is around, Gea:
      (   ) blushes
      (   ) trembles

Chapter 5

10. How did Akron and Gea return to the Underworld? What did they discover about the people in the old days?

Chapter 6

11. Why were Akron and Gea so different?

12. What feelings does Gea talk about? How does she think they can help people?

13. What are the people going to do in the Underworld?

After Reading (Optional Activities)

14. Why was Akron so curious to know what was inside the Red Zone?

15. In your opinion, will books disappear someday? Discuss with a partner the pros and cons of reading a book on printed paper and on the computer screen.

16. What are the advantages and disadvantages of computers for communication between people?